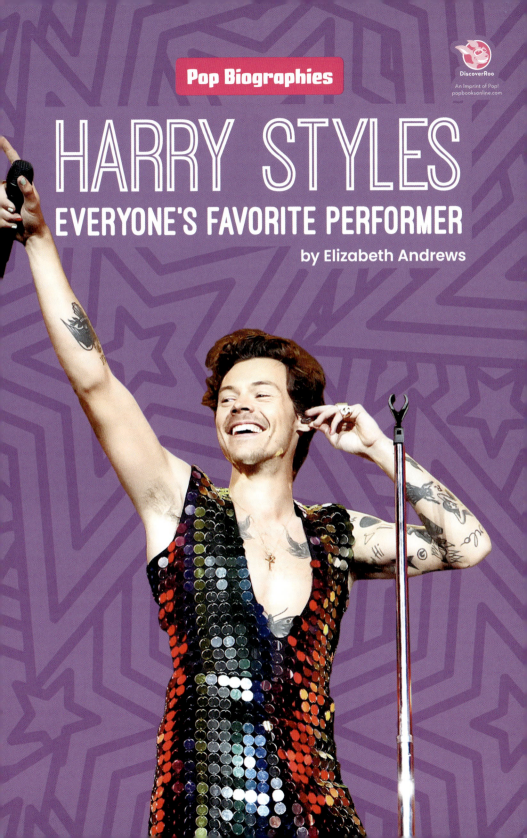

WELCOME TO
DiscoverRoo!

This book is filled with videos, puzzles, games, and more! Scan the QR codes* while you read, or visit the website below to make this book pop.

popbooksonline.com/styles

abdobooks.com

Published by Pop!, a division of ABDO, PO Box 398166, Minneapolis, Minnesota 55439. Copyright © 2024 by Abdo Consulting Group, Inc. International copyrights reserved in all countries. No part of this book may be reproduced in any form without written permission from the publisher. DiscoverRoo™ is a trademark and logo of Pop!.

Printed in the United States of America, North Mankato, Minnesota.

052023
082023

Cover Photo: Alamy Stock Photo
Interior Photos: Alamy Stock Photos, Getty Images, Shutterstock Images
Editor: Grace Hansen
Series Designer: Colleen McLaren

Library of Congress Control Number: 2022950562

Publisher's Cataloging-in-Publication Data
Names: Andrews, Elizabeth, author.
Title: Harry Styles: everyone's favorite performer / by Elizabeth Andrews
Other title: everyone's favorite performer
Description: Minneapolis, Minnesota : Pop!, 2024 | Series: Pop biographies | Includes online resources and index
Identifiers: ISBN 9781098244361 (lib. bdg.) | ISBN 9781098245061 (ebook)
Subjects: LCSH: Styles, Harry, 1994- --Juvenile literature. | Singers--Juvenile literature. | Songwriters--Juvenile literature. | Actors--Juvenile literature.
Classification: DDC 782.42166092--dc23

*Scanning QR codes requires a web-enabled smart device with a QR code reader app and a camera.

TABLE OF
CONTENTS

CHAPTER 1

HE'S GOT THE X FACTOR

Harry Edward Styles was born on February 1, 1994, in Worcestershire, England. He was raised by his mother in Holmes Chapel, Cheshire, with his older sister Gemma. Growing up, Harry worked in a bakery and played in a band with his school friends.

WATCH A VIDEO HERE!

The people of Harry's hometown were excited when he became a star.

ONE DIRECTION MEMBERS

Harry Styles

Niall Horan

Louis Tomlinson

In 2010, Harry auditioned for the British singing competition show called *The X Factor*. He made it to the second round but was **eliminated**. A judge

Simon Cowell (third from right) *has been a judge on other shows, including* American Idol.

named Simon Cowell thought Harry had

promise. So, he brought Harry back and

placed him in a group with four other

boys who had also been cut.

One Direction went on tour with contestants on The X Factor *after the season ended.*

Harry, Niall Horan, Louis Tomlinson, Zayn Malik, and Liam Payne joined together and competed on *The X Factor* as One Direction. They performed songs by Coldplay and Kelly Clarkson while on the show.

One Direction quickly gained fans during the competition. People were charmed by the group's fun attitude and goofy **antics**. One Direction didn't win their season of *The X Factor*. They came in third. But the stories of both Harry and One Direction were just beginning.

Some fans of One Direction can tell what year a photo was taken based on the boys' hairstyles.

CHAPTER 2

ONE DIRECTION INFECTION

"What Makes You Beautiful" was the first song One Direction released. It is one of the best-selling songs in boy band history. The band's first album was titled *Up All Night* and was released in November 2011.

LEARN MORE HERE!

Up All Night *has sold over five million copies.*

One Direction gained a lot of attention very quickly! The band's first tour was short. Playing at smaller **venues** allowed them to connect with their fans. But after *Up All Night* became popular, everything One Direction did got bigger.

The next album, *Take Me Home*,

was released in November 2012. Its first

single "Live While We're Young" broke the

record for fastest preordered song. Harry

was working very hard. One Direction

One Direction performed at the 2012 London Olympics!

continuously toured, made appearances, and released new albums yearly.

DID YOU KNOW? One Direction fans were called "directioners" and they knew everything about each member.

One Direction also performed at some of the award shows they attended.

In 2013, One Direction released *Midnight Memories* and announced a world stadium tour. This was the first album that had songs written by the members. It also shifted One Direction's sound from **bubblegum pop** to rock.

Four came out in November 2014. Fans were thrilled with it. In One Direction's short career, the band had been **nominated** for many awards. Fans were pleased and filled stadiums around the world. By the time the guys announced their On the Road Again tour, they were very tired.

"Steal My Girl" was the first single on Four.

Harry grew his hair long while he was in One Direction.

In February 2015, after one month on tour, Zayn left the band. Harry, Niall, Louis, and Liam stayed on tour. But in August 2015 One Direction announced the band would be going on **hiatus**. The remaining four members released one last album, *Made in the A.M.,* in November 2015.

One Direction didn't get a chance perform many songs from Made in the A.M. *on tour.*

CHAPTER 3

FLYING SOLO

After One Direction's time came to an end, Harry needed a break. He was grateful for the five years he had with the band. But it had been five years of a lot of pressure. Harry was most excited to reclaim some privacy and spend time with his family.

EXPLORE LINKS HERE!

One Direction bandmate Niall Horan helped Harry learn to play guitar.

Fans look forward to seeing what Harry will wear for each performance.

During his time off, Harry realized he missed making music. He felt ready to focus on writing music and putting together his first solo album. Within the first ten days of a writing retreat in Jamaica, six of the final ten songs of his debut solo album were written.

At concerts, Harry encourages his fans to sing along with him.

Harry Styles was released in May 2017. The album had a seventies rock and roll sound that critics enjoyed. Harry took the album on tour, playing small and big **venues**. The first **single** from the album "Sign of the Times" was **nominated** for two MTV Video Music Awards.

Harry wasn't just interested in a solo music career after One Direction. He wanted to act. His first role was in the 2017 movie *Dunkirk*. He played a young British World War II soldier named Alex.

DID YOU KNOW? On the set of the "Sign of the Times" music video, Harry hung from a helicopter 1,500 feet (457m) in the air!

Legendary singer-songwriter and rock icon Stevie Nicks was a surprise guest on Harry's first solo tour. They sang "Landslide" together.

23

CHAPTER 4

HARRY'S HOUSE

Harry's second solo album was released in December 2019. It was titled *Fine Line*. He said that making the album was about freedom. He wanted it to be fun. Unfortunately, COVID-19 prevented him from touring right away. It didn't, however, prevent anyone from enjoying the album.

COMPLETE AN ACTIVITY HERE!

Once again, critics loved the rock influence on the album. Articles and interviews mentioned the similarities Harry's music had to rock legends of the seventies.

In the fall of 2021, Harry finally got to start his Love On Tour and perform live in front of his fans. The tour would continue until July 2023.

As of January 2023, Love On Tour sold 2.6 million tickets!

Harry Styles has three Grammys, including Album of the Year and Best Pop Vocal Album. He also won Best Pop Solo Performance for "Watermelon Sugar."

DID YOU KNOW?

Harry played a 15-show **residency** at Madison Square Garden in New York for Love On Tour. He sold 277,000 tickets!

Harry's House, his third solo album, was released in May 2022. It stepped away from Harry's usual rock sounds and made something new. Harry said he thought it was his best work yet. He also said it was the most fun he's had making music. The album and its first single "As It Was" were **nominated** for six Grammys. Harry went on to win two Grammys in 2023, including the biggest award in music, Album of the Year.

STYLES' STYLE

Since his One Direction career, Harry's fashion has been applauded. As he grew up, so did his chosen looks. Harry wears big designer names like Saint Laurent and Gucci. He likes to break away from traditional male fashion. Harry's stylist uses his tour outfits to inspire fans!

Harry continued to make music and act. He had two major motion pictures come out in 2022. They were *My Policeman* and *Don't Worry Darling*. The films gave Harry the chance to grow as an actor even more.

Critics did not love My Policeman, *but Harry's fans loved it.*

Harry Styles performed with Lizzo at Coachella in 2022.

Since his start with One Direction, Harry has only grown in popularity. He has proven just how steady his star power is with each new album. Be it on stage or on the big screen, Harry Styles will shine for a long time to come.

MAKING CONNECTIONS

TEXT-TO-SELF

Have you listened to any of Harry Styles' music?
If so, what is your favorite song?

TEXT-TO-TEXT

Have you read any other books about
musicians? What did those musicians have in
common with Harry? How were they different?

TEXT-TO-WORLD

Do you think musicians have power to change
the world? Has Harry Styles changed the world?

GLOSSARY

antic — an attention-drawing, often wildly playful or funny act or action.

bubblegum pop — a type of music that is catchy and upbeat and targeted at kids, tweens, and teens.

eliminate — to put an end to or get rid of.

hiatus — a temporary break.

nominate — to choose as a possible winner for an award.

residency — a series of concerts performed at one location.

single — a song that is released as a stand-alone from an album.

venue — a place where events of a certain kind are held.

INDEX

DiscoverRoo!
ONLINE RESOURCES

This book is filled with videos, puzzles, games, and more! Scan the QR codes* while you read, or visit the website below to make this book pop.

popbooksonline.com/styles

*Scanning QR codes requires a web-enabled smart device with a QR code reader app and a camera.